· KEEPSAKE CRAFTS ·

CHRISTMAS TREE
DECORATIONS

· KEEPSAKE CRAFTS ·

CHRISTMAS
TREE
DECORATIONS

DEBORAH SCHNEEBELI-MORRELL

BCA

LONDON   NEW YORK   SYDNEY   TORONTO

A QUARTO BOOK

Copyright © 1994 Quarto Publishing plc

This edition published 1994 by BCA
by arrangement with Quarto Publishing plc
CN 5857

This book was designed and produced by
Quarto Publishing plc

Editor Joanne Jessop
Managing editor Anna Clarkson
Designers Peter Bridgewater/ Ron Bryant-
Funnell
Photographer Heini Schneebeli
Illustrator Tony Masero
Art director Moira Clinch
Editorial director Sophie Collins

Manufactured in Hong Kong by
Regent Publishing Services Ltd
Printed in China by
Leefung-Asco Printers Ltd

CONTENTS

CONTENTS

INTRODUCTION

Christmas is a special, magical celebration that helps to lift our spirits during the darkest time of the year. In almost every home the Christmas tree, with its ornaments and dazzling lights, becomes the focal point, creating a festive atmosphere that delights adults and children alike.

But shopping for decorations that suit your personal tastes and match your home decor is not an easy task, especially during the busy run-up to Christmas. It is much more rewarding to create your own special decorations. With the help of the

inspiring and inventive ideas presented in this book, you can bedeck your Christmas tree in your own unique style. Have friends and family join in on these projects to make Christmas a special time of quiet enjoyment and togetherness.

The projects in this book draw their inspiration from a rich variety of sources – from the traditional world of folk crafts to more elegant and exotic themes. The materials, too, are varied and interesting to work with. Metal foils, glittering glass beads, old bits of jewellery and scraps of colourful fabrics will add sparkle and shine to your Christmas tree decorations. Sometimes, when working with flowers or shells, the natural beauty of the materials themselves will inspire the design. In other projects, some very ordinary household objects, such as scouring pads, are put to extraordinary uses with stunning results.

These festive Christmas tree decorations could become treasured additions to your family collection or lovely gifts with a personal touch.

7

MATERIALS

Many of the projects in this book have been inspired by the exciting and inventive work of folk artists from less technically sophisticated cultures than our own. The book aims to encourage the reader to be resourceful, to be inspired by everyday objects and to transform ordinary materials into lovely and unusual decorations. It is a good idea to build up a rich and varied collection of materials; to some extent the availability of materials will dictate your style and, therefore, how your work will look. Many of the materials used in this book are quite readily available, either from haberdashers, art suppliers or even your own collection of discarded items - nothing is more rewarding than recycling throw away objects into beautiful and useful things.

Hobby or specialist bead shops have an amazing choice of products from all over the world, as well as wire and thread.

Once you have gathered together enough simple materials for a few of the projects, let your imagination loose and enjoy yourself, whilst discovering new ways of using materials and simple techniques.

METAL FOIL

The metal foil used for the repoussé work in the first six projects is really the only material that needs to be bought from a specialist source, such as a sheet metal supplier, although some may be available from good craft or art shops. Kitchen aluminium foil is much too thin, but if you do have difficulties finding the right metal foil, aluminium take-away or frozen food containers could be used. Another substitute is opened out aluminium drinks cans - but always take care when cutting metal and beware of sharp corners.

FABRIC AND RIBBONS

The fabric projects all use small scraps of rather vivid and lustrous materials saved from dressmaking, cut from old clothes or even found in a dressing-up box. The effect of appliquéd contrasting fabric with simple sequinned and beaded embroidery is quite stunning, especially when crowned with brightly coloured feathers plucked deftly from a feather duster (see the embroidered birds project on page 24).

Short lengths of exotic ribbon, brightly coloured or luxuriant to the touch, can have stunning effects and are cheap to buy in very small quantities.

For the bird project (page 24), the sparkling stars project (page 26) and the luscious leaves project (page 28), small amounts of polyester padding were used to lightly stuff the decorations. You could also use nylon stockings or tights.

BUTTONS AND BEADS

Nearly every household has some small tins and boxes, perhaps hidden at the back of a drawer, containing old buttons and beads. Supplement this collection with a variety of new buttons and beads of all shapes and sizes, including coloured glass and plastic crystals, tear drop pearls, little seed beads and pressed metal charms. Always look out for exciting and unusual items when you are shopping, even if you are not making anything in particular at the time; you never know when you will need something really special.

JEWELS

Old or unwanted cheap jewellery is a good way of making a tree decoration look particularly exotic and resplendent. Look out for this in junk shops or at jumble sales; some good haberdashers may sell flat backed jewels. The little mirrors in the curly metal frames (page 20) come from a dolls' house shop.

PAPIER MÂCHÉ

Papier-mâché pulp is a very versatile medium that was used to model the frosted fruit project (page 29), the brilliant birds (page 30) and the little painted animals (page 32). It has also been used as a backing for the dazzling dangles (page 42), and the tree-topper stars (pages 61-2). It is widely available as a proprietary pulp mix from craft or toy shops, and is inexpensive when used in small quantities. You may even like to make your own pulp, especially if you enjoy working in this medium. The recipe is on page 29.

PAPERS AND WRAPPINGS

A wide variety of brightly coloured papers, glittery sweet wrappers, coloured tissue paper and hand-printed Indian papers has been used in the découpage-inspired projects, baubles galore (page 38) and the glittering faceted star (page 62). Build up your own supply by saving gift wrap, chocolate or Easter egg wrappers and anything else that catches your eye; it may be just what you will need one day.

NATURAL ITEMS

If you go for walks in woods, fields or along the seashore, don't miss the chance to collect unusual items. Seeds, pine cones, shells and poppy seed heads are all used in the projects on pages 48-50. Those you can't find, you can buy from specialist shops.

GLUES, PAINTS AND VARNISH

Four different types of glue are used in this book, and all are easily available - white PVA glue, clear glue, epoxy glue and a cellulose paste for the découpage projects.

The paints in the book are all acrylic or gouache. Both types are water-based and both dry quickly to an opaque and water-fast finish. Polyurethane varnish is used on the salt-dough projects (page 54).

BASIC TECHNIQUES

All the projects provide guidelines and practical tips for creating stunning decorations. But this is only the starting point; in each case there are endless possibilities to be explored. The aim of this book is to spark your creative talents and encourage you to experiment with other techniques and materials to invent your own personal designs.

No special technical ability is necessary for these projects, and they can all be made at home using simple everyday tools. Many projects use leftover materials such as sweet wrappers and old newspapers that you might have saved.

1 For the sewing projects you can use lovely scraps of fabric, ribbons, buttons, sequins and brightly coloured feathers plucked from a feather duster. You need only the most rudimentary sewing and embroidery skills. The success and quality of the decorations lies not so much in the skill of the maker, but more in the clever and inventive use of materials.

2 For some projects, particularly the repoussé metal decorations and the painted tin animals, you will need sheet metal foil from a good craft shop or sheet metal supplier. These materials are surprisingly easy to work with. The metal is thin and cuts easily with scissors.

3 You can even draw on it, or trace designs from this book if you do not feel confident in your own drawing skills.

4 Papier-mâché pulp is used in several projects. You can use a proprietary brand of paper pulp or you may prefer to make your own from the recipe on page 29.

5 Some projects require simple craft techniques that most people have tried, such as découpage, painting and modelling in papier mâché.

6 Nimble fingers and a little patience are all that are needed for the simpler projects such as the pomanders. And what could be simpler than tying bows and stringing beads together?

REPOUSSÉ METAL SHAPES

The stunning effect of
these lovely glittering metal
ornaments belies the
simplicity of their
making.

This lightweight metal foil is thin enough to be cut with an ordinary pair of scissors; the relief of repoussé work is created by drawing on the back of the metal with a dry ballpoint pen. You can use soft-drink cans if you cannot find any metal foil.

The metal foils used here are brass, copper, aluminium and phosphor bronze foils. Foils are very thin metal sheeting. If you feel confident, draw the outline of your design directly onto the back of the metal with a soft pencil. Place the metal on a soft surface – an old magazine will do; now draw, pressing very heavily with a ballpoint pen over your pencil lines. Draw some freehand patterns – faces, stars, hearts, etc. – within the outline. Cut out the design with scissors and make a hole at the top for hanging.

Watch these metal shapes shine at night when the tree is all lit up.

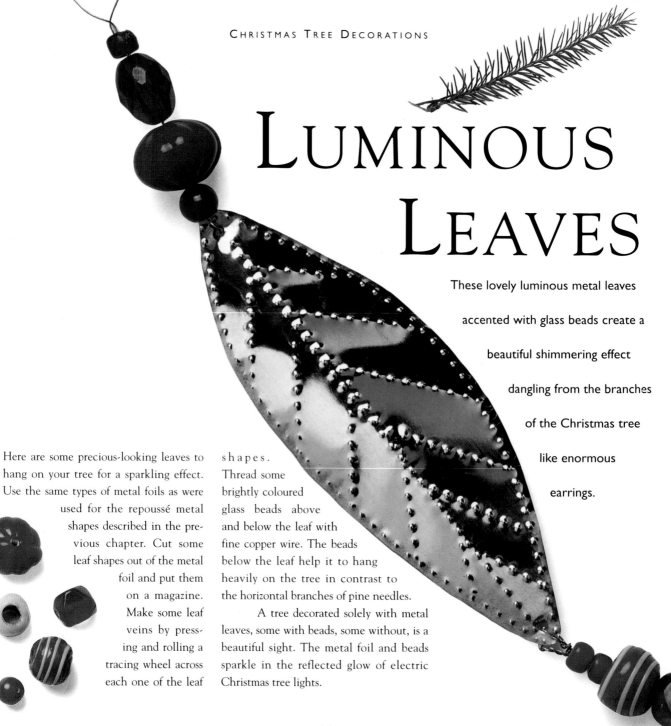

LUMINOUS LEAVES

These lovely luminous metal leaves accented with glass beads create a beautiful shimmering effect dangling from the branches of the Christmas tree like enormous earrings.

Here are some precious-looking leaves to hang on your tree for a sparkling effect. Use the same types of metal foils as were used for the repoussé metal shapes described in the previous chapter. Cut some leaf shapes out of the metal foil and put them on a magazine. Make some leaf veins by pressing and rolling a tracing wheel across each one of the leaf shapes. Thread some brightly coloured glass beads above and below the leaf with fine copper wire. The beads below the leaf help it to hang heavily on the tree in contrast to the horizontal branches of pine needles.

A tree decorated solely with metal leaves, some with beads, some without, is a beautiful sight. The metal foil and beads sparkle in the reflected glow of electric Christmas tree lights.

14

You can make all the leaves with one type of metal foil as shown here, or you can try using several different types of foil. Choose the metals to match the style of your tree. Copper and bronze have a warmer feel to them; on the other hand, aluminium leaves accentuated with silver or pearl beads create a much cooler, more wintery effect.

You might like to experiment by painting some of the metal leaves with transparent glass paints as discussed in the next project.

Make a lovely garland for your tree by stringing the metal leaves together on a thin copper wire and interspersing them with glass beads.

These

shiny

metal leaves

make stunning

tree decorations.

Luminous leaves

can be made in a

great variety of

shapes and sizes

from several types

of metal foil.

METAL MENAGERIE

These charming little animals made from copper or aluminium foil are

inspired by the popular tin decorations from Mexico.

Cut out simple animal shapes and draw patterns on the back with a ball-point pen.

Transparent glass paints can be used to great effect on these metal figures; the metal sheen glimmering through the paint is very arresting. When the paint is thoroughly dry, you could try lightly rubbing the raised drawn lines with very fine sandpaper to reveal the glinting metal beneath.

The cornucopia, fish and vase with flowers were made in the same way and painted with opaque enamel paints. Matt or shiny paint can be used.

Transparent glass

paints can give an

extra sheen to a

colourful metal

menagerie.

There are endless possibilities for these decorations; visit museums and galleries or look in art and craft books for inspiration.

HEAVENLY SHAPES

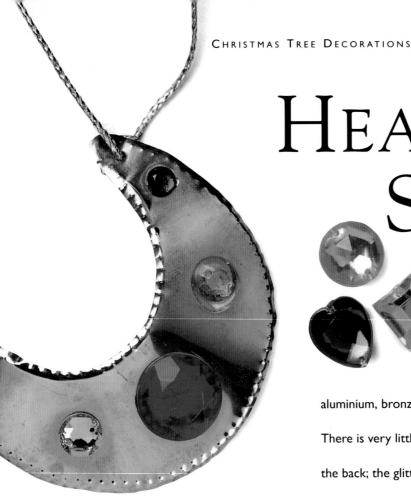

These simple shapes – moons, stars and flowers – have been cut out of aluminium, bronze and copper foil. There is very little repoussé work on the back; the glittering effect is created by adding flat-backed "jewels".

The crescent moon was edged from the back of the foil with a tracing wheel to create an even line of little raised dots on the front. Brightly coloured "jewels" with different-sized facets were added to create a regal feel. Most clear adhesives are strong enough to hold the "jewels" in place.

This gold star has a large, imitation cut-diamond in the middle, surrounded by shimmering pearls.

The aluminium flower has a large jewel in the centre with smaller ones on each petal to complement it.

The embellishments are your choice, depending on what is available.

Whatever you decide to use, the combination of the reflective metal and the glittering jewels is a winner.

MINIATURE
MIRRORS
& JEWELS

These miniature framed mirrors

are inspired by Indian

embroidery, in which lots of

tiny mirrors are sewn into a

piece of fabric to give it a

wonderfully rich and

sparkling texture.

Cut the mirror frames out of the metal foil and draw some repoussé designs on the back, perhaps to frame the mirror or decorate the hanging tab.

The curly effect is produced by simply cutting the metal frame into very thin strips all around the outside. If the strips are cut thin enough, the metal will automatically curl into this unusual border. Stick your mirror onto the centre of the frame with a strong epoxy glue. You can find small round, oval or rectangular mirrors in most doll's house shops. Glue some little seed pearls or glass beads around the mirror to disguise the join.

You may prefer to have a large jewel in the centre of the frame instead of a mirror.

Try hanging these miniature mirrors on your lit-up tree. Turn off the house lights and watch the mirrors throw their magical reflections about the darkened room.

The tiny mirrors in the centre of these decorations add radiance and sparkle to any Christmas tree.

Metal figures can
be put to several
uses, as wreath
decorations, crib
figures, gift tags,
and, of course,
Christmas tree
ornaments.

METAL FIGURES

This man and the woman on the opposite page are roughly based on images of the seventeenth-century pilgrims who founded the American colonies.

You can really go to town working on the back of these metal figures with a dry ballpoint pen. Don't forget to pierce a hole in the top for suspending the little figures from the tree.

Why not make a whole family and their animals? What about Noah and his Ark? Or a nativity scene? This little angel could be one of your crib figures.

Metal figures look lovely pinned onto the front door at Christmas, or perhaps fixed to a festive wreath. Smaller figures could be made as gift tags, with the name of the recipient on each one. Remember you must write backwards so that the words will read correctly from the front.

This sturdy little character was given lots of interesting features by drawing on the back with a ballpoint pen.

EMBROIDERED BIRDS

What is more appropriate than to have a flock of birds settle on a tree? Perhaps these visitors have come from more exotic lands to brighten up our winters.

Bits of fabric can be fashioned into whimsical birds.

24

These unusual little birds, made from scraps of fabric and glittering ribbons, are embroidered with small seed beads and shining sequins. Little assorted packets of colourful sequins are readily available in most haberdashery stores.

Use small pieces of fabric: the more exotic the better. Try gold lamé, shot silk, or diaphanous netting material. Draw a very simple bird-shaped body onto double thickness of fabric and cut it out slightly larger to take account of the seam. Sew the pieces together, right sides facing, and leave a small opening for the padding. Turn right side out, fill with padding, and sew up the hole. Appliqué small contrasting bits of fabric for the wings and embroider with beads and sequins. Add some ribbons. For the tails, you can use brightly coloured feathers. Always make sure the eyes stand out.

The Scottish tartan bird with diamanté eyes has a crown and tail made from the same thin red ribbon that decoratively binds the body.

Gold tassels, small bells or a rich combination of beads hanging under the bird make an interesting addition.

25

This star and these little parcels are made with colourful fabrics and then embellished with bright ribbons and braided sequins.

SPARKLING STARS & PRECIOUS PARCELS

Stars hold a very special significance at Christmas. It was a gleaming star that led the Three Kings from far-off lands to the humble stable in Bethlehem where Christ was born on Christmas day. Stars hanging on our Christmas tree remind us of the star of Bethlehem.

These sparkling stars and precious little parcels are very easy to sew. Just cut out a star or parcel shape from a double thickness of fabric, remembering to add the seam allowance. Choose a variety of fabrics, perhaps ones that are richly patterned or have an antique look. You could also try shimmering and tinselly fabrics.

With the fabric right sides together, neatly sew around the shape, leaving a small opening. Turn the fabric right side out and stuff loosely. Insert a hanging loop before sewing up the opening.

Then go to town on the decorations, adding sequins and beads. Tie the parcels with colourful ribbons and bows. Cross the star with narrow ribbons and stud with starry sequins. Perhaps you could even add little jingling bells on each point of the star. Try hanging tassels from the three lower points of the star.

Tassels are easy to make. Simply wrap a small skein of metallic thread around your fingers, remove, and bind one end of the skein with the same thread. Cut the other end to form the tassel.

These delightful ornaments are easy to make; all you need is some fabric and glitter and lots of imagination.

This richly patterned red star with its shiny gold tassels would be a delightful feature on your Christmas tree.

LUSCIOUS LEAVES & FLOWERS

These leaves and flowers are very easy to make and so effective as Christmas ornaments. The pearly flower is made like a little cushion with a pleated silver ribbon edge. The grey silk centre of the flower was decorated with a collection of old and new pearl buttons to signify seeds and then circled with a twinkling row of tiny pearls.

Use rich dark velvet to make the leaves. Cut a double layer of fabric into simple leaf shapes; be sure to include the seam allowances. Try using a contrasting colour for the back of the leaf. With the right sides of the fabric facing together, sew around the leaf, leaving one end open. Turn right side out, stuff loosely, and, after inserting a hanging loop, sew up the open end. Use metallic thread to embroider the front with leaf veins. Pinpoint the ends of the veins with little seed pearls. As a variation, use long silvery beads to accentuate the leaf motif and finish with tiny iridescent seed beads. Finally, bind the hanging end of the leaves with matching metallic thread.

28

FROSTED FRUITS

These fruits were modelled in papier mâché and allowed to dry thoroughly before being primed with a thick white primer and painted a rich, ripe fruit colour. When the paint was dry, a little gold powder was dusted over the surface.

Those lovely curling tendrils on the grapes are very easy to make from copper foil, which curls naturally when it is cut into thin strips.

Although proprietary pulp is available from craft or good toy shops, you may enjoy making your own from this recipe.

Tear a newspaper into small squares and boil in plenty of water until the paper begins to disintegrate. Allow to cool, then mash with a potato masher. Strain off excess water and squeeze dry. Add half a cup of PVA adhesive, a sprinkling of dry cellulose or starch paste, half a cup of proprietary wall filler and one cup of fine sawdust. Knead energetically until all the ingredients are well mixed. This pulp mixture will keep for a number of weeks in the refrigerator.

These little gold-dusted fruits are modelled out of papier-mâché pulp; the leaves are made from copper foil, which is pushed into the pulp fruit while it is still soft.

You could make a variety of fruit and create a riot of shimmering colours to decorate your tree.

29

BRILLIANT BIRDS

These brilliantly painted birds are modelled from papier-mâché pulp, and, as with the frosted fruit, the metal wings and crowns are inserted into the pulp before it begins to dry. Remember to make a hole through the bird at this stage to accommodate a hanging loop.

The metal foil can be folded like a fan, cut into strips or tightly curled. For an unusual effect you can hold the metal crown and tail over a naked flame for a moment so that they take on a lustrous patination. The pretty white bird shown above has a tail and crown made from an unravelled aluminium scouring pad.

When the pulp is thoroughly dry, prime the birds and then paint them with bright acrylic or gouache paints.

Finally, add coloured glitter to make the birds sparkle on the tree.

These bright little papier-mâché birds

are adorned with metallic

crowns and tails.

Try putting a little rider or acrobat on the horse, or make a sleigh for the reindeer to pull.

32

LITTLE PAINTED ANIMALS

These charming little animals are inspired by the carved and

painted wooden toys made in India.

Start by making an internal framework of pipe cleaners and fix it to a cardboard base with strong glue. Model the papier-mâché pulp around the framework to create an animal form – a horse, a fox or a reindeer. Insert a little loop of wire into the back of the animal and paper the base over with pasted newspaper strips. After it is thoroughly dry and primed, paint the animals in the manner of naive folk art, sometimes leaving the white primer to show as a contrast to the bright colour. Add patterns, dots and stripes, using colours that clash or dazzle.

These decorations employ the

most commonly used method of

making papier mâché.

CRACKERS, STOCKINGS & CROWNS

First, cut the shapes from thin cardboard and carefully cover them all over with pasted news-paper. Remember to insert a small wire hook at this stage. When the paper is dry, prime the pieces and paint them with bright colours. Glue on some glittering wrapping paper or sweet wrappers.

Motifs from a gold doily enhance the red and gold theme of the Christmas cracker shown above.

The majestic gold

crown in the

window looks

splendid with its

twinkling jewels;

gold glitter around

the edge finishes it

off in style.

Engraving on

painted baubles

produces some

intriguing designs

with a very

professional look.

Engraved baubles are a real pleasure to make. Wrap polystyrene balls with two layers of pasted paper and allow to dry before priming with two coats of white primer. Push a chopstick into one end of the ball to provide a handle and then start painting the ball with some brightly coloured designs. When you remove the stick, the hole can be filled with glue to hold the hanging loop, which is a length of gold pipe cleaner threaded with a bright glass bead

When the paint is dry, add some finer details to your designs by carefully scratching out a pattern to reveal the white primer beneath the paint. Use a sharp pointed instrument, such as the blade of a craft knife.

This engraving process is a traditional technique used in Switzerland to decorate Easter eggs. As you can see from the baubles shown here, the final effect is very attractive and professional looking. People are always intrigued with these engraved baubles and want to know how they were made.

PAINTED & ENGRAVED BAUBLES

These painted and engraved baubles make a spirited change from the traditional glass balls that usually hang on the Christmas tree.

Save your Christmas gift wrapping

paper and use it to make next year's

baubles. This is one of the

quickest and most rewarding

projects in the book.

BAUBLES
GALORE

The continuous surface of a

sphere provides enormous

scope for decorating ideas.

To make these colourful and decorative baubles, first paper some polystyrene balls with an array of different background colours. Then, using old bits of wrapping paper, sweet wrappers, sequins, pearl-headed pins, glitter, some metallic thread and lots of imagination, make a whole range of dazzling baubles. You could try some of the various techniques used to make the baubles shown here. Dot the bauble with flower-shaped sequins and fix them on with small pearl-headed pins. Découpage motifs can be cut out of beautiful hand-printed paper from India. To add glittering silver stars, first paint some glue stars on the bauble and then sprinkle them with glitter. Sweet wrappers cut into strips are ideal for creating glittering striped baubles. Bits of torn-up shiny paper can be glued in between the stripes for added interest. Try binding some metallic thread over natural handmade papers or over scrunched-up coloured tissue paper.

There is no end to the variety of attractive baubles you can make using odd bits of paper and some glittery embellishments.

MINIATURE CHURCH & HOUSES

These are buildings straight out of a fairy tale. Try making a whole village or the witch's cottage from the story of Hansel and Gretel.

These buildings are very simple to assemble from thin pieces of cardboard. The ones shown here were made from pizza boxes.

Look for ideas and inspiration in magazines, picture books and particularly travel catalogues. Make a simple house shape by sticking the cardboard together with PVA adhesive; use small strips of masking tape to hold the cardboard pieces in place while the glue dries, then paste thin paper all over the little building. Allow it to dry, then prime and paint with bright colours. Add sequins, glitter and fine braid to finish.

This miniature church and quaint little houses are modelled on decorative buildings of Eastern Europe.

DAZZLING DANGLES

These dazzling dangles are modelled out of papier mâché. The glittering jewels in the centre are added while the pulp base is still soft and moist.

Model some stars, crescents, diamonds, hearts and circles from papier mâché. While they are still soft, push a large, flat-backed faceted jewel into the centre of each shape. The paper pulp will conveniently shrink a little when drying and hold the jewel firmly in place.

You can use any type of costume jewellery to make these dangles. This would be a good use for those old pieces of jewellery that you no longer wear. Anything that glitters will give a lovely effect as a centrepiece for your ornaments.

Broken antique blue and white china shards can also be used instead of jewels. The dangles shown here were made with bits of eighteenth-century English china. The eccentric shape of the shard will dictate the way the pulp is modelled around it.

While the pulp is still soft, pierce a hole in it for the hanging loop. If you want to string a few of the dangles together, don't forget to add little loops of wire at the top and bottom of each shape. If they are to hang singly, then just one loop at the top of the dangle will do.

When the pulp is dry, carefully paint around the china or jewel with gold paint. For a really lustrous effect, add precious metal leaf on top. You can buy books of silver, gold, copper, aluminium or even patinated metal leaf quite cheaply. It sticks readily to varnish that is just tacky and nearly dry. The final effect can be quite stunning.

Using odd bits of

broken china adds

interesting textures

and shapes.

43

BEADS, BELLS
& BOWS

These stylish, elegant decorations are quick and

simple to make, but you need to be bold and

extravagant.

Use large beads and chandelier-type drop crystals for these tree ornaments. The ones shown here are made with a combination of large Indian pressed-metal beads and imitation crystals, which come in a range of colours and are much cheaper than glass crystals.

Work out your colour scheme carefully, perhaps adding little glass beads of a contrasting colour between the crystal and metal beads. It is best to use thin copper or silver wire for threading; this is available in craft or bead shops. Complete your decorations with an elegant flourish, such as a matching bow at the top of the beads.

44

RESPLENDENT RINGS

Ringed decorations

embellished with

beads and bows,

are an interesting

variation on hanging glass beads.

You could also try

threading beads

onto the wire ring

as shown below.

You can buy hoops or wire rings from jewellery suppliers or bead shops, or simply make your own from silver wire. Hang a combination of pressed metal and glittering glass beads from the bottom of the ring.

To make the ribbon rings, first pad the wire ring with polyester to create some thickness before tightly wrapping it with ribbon.

The ribbon ring on the right was finished with a pink organdie bow to pick up the iridescence in the crystal beads. The other two rings have gleaming gold bows to accent their blue and gold theme.

LARGE BEADED TASSELS

This golden tassel

was designed for a

large ostentatious

Christmas tree.

Gold tassels have an opulent and palatial feel

about them, and these simple beaded tassels

have a restrained but glorious effect. Yet both

are deceptively simple to make.

Try making a more unusual tassel, like the one shown opposite in gauzy lilac organdie. It is tightly bound at the top with gold thread and threaded above with gold beads. A beautiful bronze ruched ribbon tipped with a modest lilac bow gives an elegant finishing touch.

The large tassel shown on the left is suspended from a gold-sprayed ball flecked with gold leaf. A rosette of metallic woven ribbon tops it off beautifully.

46

SHELL ORNAMENTS

The natural world is full of inspiration for the artist. What object could have more exquisite perfection and beauty than a seashell, with its extraordinary spiral forms and the natural iridescence of its pearly surface? The tree ornaments shown on these pages use pearl droplets, beads and ribbons to accentuate the natural beauty and charm of seashells.

Seashell ornaments have an aura of glistening purity, like hanging icicles.

Shell ornaments are ideal for the under-stated tree with pale, subtle colours. Use them in combination with white, silver or pearly decorations and your tree will take on an other-worldly quality.

Interesting shells are widely available, either in gift or specialist shell shops and they are not generally expensive. Choose a collection of examples that complement each other.

Seashells are quite soft, so it is easy to drill little holes into them with a small bradawl or drill. Suspend droplet pearls, silver stars, crystals, silver lockets or little bunches of bells from silver wire threaded through the holes. Use ruched ribbons or polka-dot net-ting to complete the decoration.

NUTS & SEEDS

We can only wonder at the incredible world of nature with its wealth of intricate design. Walnuts, which are of course already designed to hang from a tree, are even more beautiful when sprayed with gold or silver paint.

Nuts,

pine cones,

seed heads and

cinnamon sticks

make naturally

beautiful

ornaments.

To embellish the natural design of nuts and seed heads, hang little metal charms beneath them. You could also quarter a walnut with shining red braid and top it with a matching plume of brightly coloured feathers for a whimsical touch.

Alternatively, cut a walnut in half, scoop out the nut and line the inside with luscious fabric. Then glue a gleaming jewel in the centre and little seed pearls around the edge to form a natural heart shape. Hang the nut shell from the tree with red braid attached with a little rosette.

50

Spray a pine cone gold and top it with a gold bow and hanging loop. Or you could try painting the cones red or green and then adding glitter to the tips. Finish them with little tartan ribbon rosettes and matching braid hanging loops.

A poppy seed head makes an ideal Christmas tree ornament. Spray it gold, then pierce a little hole in the stem and fill it with glue. Insert a hanging loop that has been threaded with one or two glistening glass beads.

A little bunch of cinnamon sticks tied together with gold braid and a tassel is very evocative of the winter season.

When out on country walks, look for interesting nuts and seeds that you could use for tree decorations. With an inventive mind and creative combinations, the variety of ornaments you can make is limitless.

A cinnamon stick ornament gives off a delicious scent.

POMANDERS

Everybody knows of the Elizabethan pomander – an orange,

preserved and studded with spicily scented cloves. But there are

many alternatives to this old

favourite. Some are very simple

to make, and they are all

quite lovely.

These pomanders

could be scented

with a spicy

Christmas pot-

pourri essence.

For the shell pomander, quarter a polystyrene ball with gold ribbon and fix the tiny seashells inside each quarter with PVA adhesive. To help keep the shells in place while the adhesive is drying, make a little fence of dressmaking pins around the inside edge of the ribbon that defines the quarter you are working on. For neatness, fix all the shells in one direction. When the ball is completely covered, make a rosette with the same ribbon, then push the rosette and a hanging loop into a small glued hole at the top of the pomander. The rosebud and white helicrysum pomanders couldn't be simpler. Just push the pointed stem of the flowers in to an oasis ball, which is available from any florist.

SALT DOUGH

Salt dough is another traditional favourite for

Christmas decorations. And it is

particularly suitable for children, as

long as they don't try to eat it!

Salt-dough ornaments can be left in their natural state or painted with vibrant colours.

The basic recipe for salt dough is 2 cups of all-purpose flour and 1 cup of salt. Add water gradually to the dry ingredients until the mixture is stiff, but not sticky, then knead for about ten minutes until it is smooth and manageable.

Working on a floured board, shape wreaths, hearts and baskets of flowers out of the dough. Use bits of dough to add interesting details and embellishments. Make a hole through the top of the dough figure for threading a ribbon, or just glue the ribbon onto the back.

When you have made your shapes, allow them to dry thoroughly over a few days. A warm oven may help for a short time, but take care not to cook them or they will yellow.

Varnish some of the shapes in their natural colour. Paint others with vivid colours to look like South American salt-dough decorations. Varnish these as well to enhance the colour.

CHRISTMAS COOKIES

Every Christmas, some Europeans make delicious spicy

cookies in a great abundance to give to visitors during the

holiday season. Cookies can also be used as festive

Christmas tree decorations.

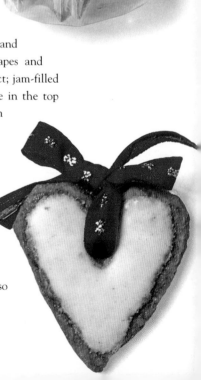

Tie some cookies

onto the tree with

pretty ribbons, or,

to keep them really

fresh, pack a few

cookies into a

cellophane

bunch and tie

it onto the tree.

There are many flavours and shapes of Christmas cookies – wreath-shaped aniseed cookies; cinnamon and almond cookies cut into simple shapes and iced before baking for a glazed effect; jam-filled shortbread sandwiches with a hole in the top layer to reveal the jam centre. Try adapting your favourite recipes to create some interesting variations.

Cut out the cookies in different shapes – stars, hearts, diamonds, Christmas trees. Try the Swiss technique of pressing the dough into moulds so that it takes up the relief picture.

GARLANDS

Garlands provide a wonderful contrast to the vertically

hung decorations. A tree lavishly swagged and

looped with glorious garlands is a spectacle

to behold. Here are some ideas to spark

your imagination.

Garlands can be

made with everyday

objects such as

scouring pads and

packing chips.

Gold and silver

paint or sequins

produce some

stunning effects.

58

Golden ribbons and glass beads create an exquisite-looking garland for your Christmas tree.

Unravel a silver or copper scouring pad and slot in little pink and red starred sequins. You might like to use dried flowers or little shells instead of sequins. One pad will stretch for about a metre, so you may need a few to decorate a tree.

Here is a way to put polystyrene packing chips to a good use. Spray them gold and silver and thread them together in an interesting pattern, then loop the garland around your tree for a spectacular effect.

For a softer look, sew together a length of golden ribbon bows. You can sew little glass beads between the bows.

Chinese lanterns make a colourful garland. String the lanterns together with thin copper wire or nylon string, threading shells and beads in between each lantern.

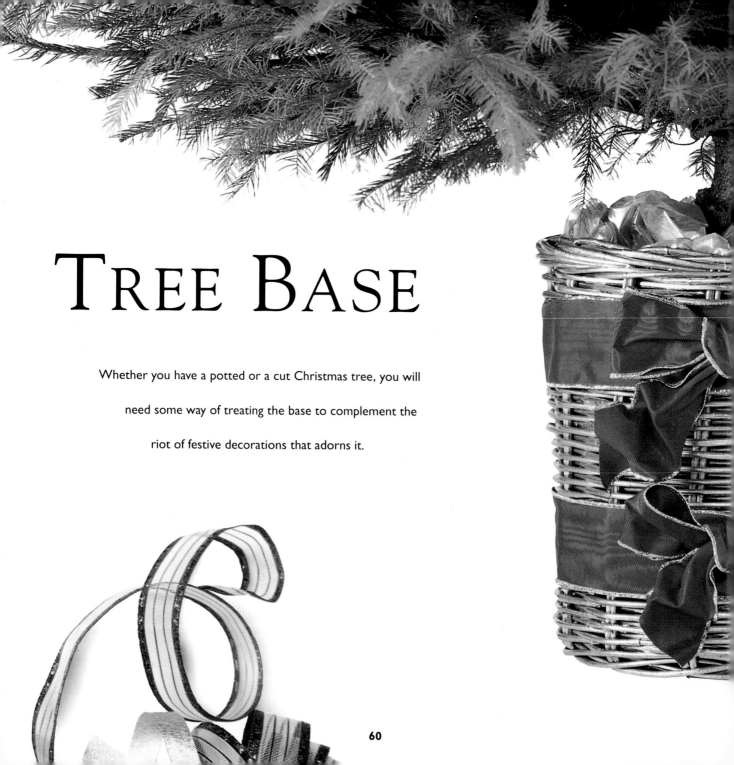

TREE BASE

Whether you have a potted or a cut Christmas tree, you will

need some way of treating the base to complement the

riot of festive decorations that adorns it.

Your live tree may come already pot planted. If not, plant it firmly in a generous-sized pot; clay or plastic will do equally well. If you are using a cut tree, wedge it securely into a flower pot with logs and pour sand in the pot to make it solid. Be sure to line the pot with a plastic bag so that the sand does not leak out.

The tree base shown here was made by decorating a straight-sided basket large enough to hold the pot. The basket was first sprayed silver and then spatter sprayed with gold paint to give it a rich gold and silver effect. Scrunched-up iridescent paper was arranged loosely on top of the flower pot around the tree trunk to create a really sumptuous base for the tree. Two wired ribbons with luscious bows tied at the front were wrapped around the basket. Wired ribbon can be easily pushed into shape and stays in place on the basket. The purple ribbon with its gold trim is a perfect complement to the gold-flecked basket and the iridescent paper .

The charm of a well-decorated tree

begins at the base. A basket tree

container can be beautifully

decorated to tie in with the

overall theme of the rest of your tree.

TREE TOPPERS

Crowning the top of the Christmas tree is the climax of all your tree decorating achievements.

A star is the traditional tree topper. Here are some ideas for stars that will top your richly decorated tree with a spectacular flourish.

To make your Christmas tree star, start by cutting the basic star shape out of a thick piece of cardboard. Model the faceted side of the star with paper pulp. Do this on both sides of the cardboard base. While the paper pulp is still soft and moist, insert a substantial piece of wire into one of the points of the star; curl the wire into a loose spiral. This will hold your star on the topmost branch of the tree. When the pulp is thoroughly dry, paper over the star.

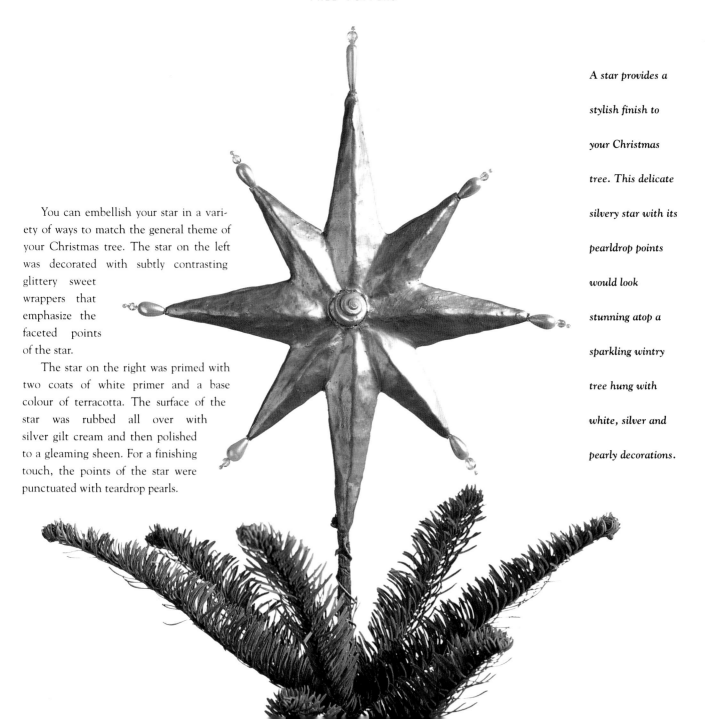

A star provides a stylish finish to your Christmas tree. This delicate silvery star with its pearldrop points would look stunning atop a sparkling wintry tree hung with white, silver and pearly decorations.

You can embellish your star in a variety of ways to match the general theme of your Christmas tree. The star on the left was decorated with subtly contrasting glittery sweet wrappers that emphasize the faceted points of the star.

The star on the right was primed with two coats of white primer and a base colour of terracotta. The surface of the star was rubbed all over with silver gilt cream and then polished to a gleaming sheen. For a finishing touch, the points of the star were punctuated with teardrop pearls.

ACKNOWLEDGEMENTS

The author would like to thank Fenella Brown for her contributions to this book on p. 16, pp. 18-19, p. 26 (little parcels), p. 29, pp. 34-35, pp. 38-39 (some of the baubles), p. 44 (beaded bow, left), p. 45 (ring, left), p. 46, p. 52 (rosebud pomander), pp. 58-59 (gold and silver garland, ribbon and bow garland). She would also like to thank Heini Schneebeli for his lovely, clear photographs.